Learn to

Arabic

Simple method for beginners

Nabat Pub © 2023

This book belongs to:

Table of Contents

1- Introduction

- The Arabic language is read and written from right to left.

Example: the word "house" in English, which is written from left to right, is written "كِتَاب" in Arabic, starting from the right and moving to the left. كِتَاب

- The forms of Arabic letters change depending on their position in the word. For example, the letter "ك" can have an initial form at the beginning of a word: " كـ ", a medial form in the middle of a word: "ـكـ", and a final form at the end of a word: "ـك".

- Arabic letters do not have a distinction between lowercase and uppercase.

- The Arabic alphabet consists only of consonants.
For example: the letter [ك] represents the sound [k].

2 - Diacritics.

To be able to pronounce the words in Arabic, we must add to the basic letters the diacritics, called harakaat (حَرَكَات), which are independent of the alphabet.

2.1 - Short vowels.

Fatha : ◌َ which gives the sound [a].

kasra : ◌ِ which gives the sound [i].

Damma : ◌ُ which gives the sound [u].

Example:

فَ	=	[fa]
فِ	=	[fi]
فُ	=	[fu]

2.2 Long vowels

- The sound [aa] which is extended orally and in writing by the letter "l".

- The sound [ii] which is extended orally and in writing by the letter "ﻴ / ي".

- The sound [uu] which is extended orally and in writing by the letter "و".

Example:

		فا	=	[faa]
في	=	فيـ	=	[fii]
		فـو	=	[fuu]

2.3 Tanwiin.

Tanwin indicates the presence of a pronounced "n" after the vowel.

Example:

فً	=	[fa] + [n]
فٍ	=	[fi] + [n]
فٌ	=	[fu] + [n]

2.4 Sukuun.

Sukuun "ْ" : is a diacritical mark representing the absence of a vowel and producing a pure consonant.

Example:

فْ	=	[f]

2.5 Shadda.

Shadda "ّ" indicates that the consonant is pronounced with increased force, giving the sound a distinct intensity.

فَّ	=	[ffa]
فِّ	=	[ffi]
فُّ	=	[ffu]

7

3. Table of the letters of the Arabic alphabet.

Letter	Description	Transliteration
ء	Glottal stop like the sound preceding a word beginning with a vowel, as in "at " or "out"	**a**
ب	"b" in "ball".	**b**
ت	"t" in "tomato"	**t**
ث	th in "thanks".	**th**
ج	"j" in "jam"	**j**
ح	Produced by saying "ha" while constricting throat muscles.	**h**
خ	"j" Spanish in "juguete".	**kh**
د	"d" in "door".	**d**
ذ	"th" in " the" or "that".	**dh**
ر	"r" in "rap"	**R**
ز	"z" in "zero".	**z**
س	"s" in "saturday".	**s**
ش	"sh" in " share".	**ch**

ص	Emphatic counterpart of "s / س", similar to the "s" in "sauce".	S
ض	Emphatic counterpart of "د / d".	ḍ
ط	Emphatic counterpart of "ت / t".	T
ظ	Emphatic counterpart of "the / ض".	ẓ
ع	It is described as a cyclic consonant or a pharyngeal contraction.	'
غ	The French "r".	r
ف	"f " in "four".	f
ق	Like "k" in "kiwi", but pronounced from the back of the throat.	q
ک = ك	"k" in "kiwi"	k
ل	"l" in "life"	l
م	"m" in "mather"	m
ن	"n" in "nine"	n
ھ = ه	"h" in "hello"	H
و	"w" in "win"	w
ي	"y in "you"	y

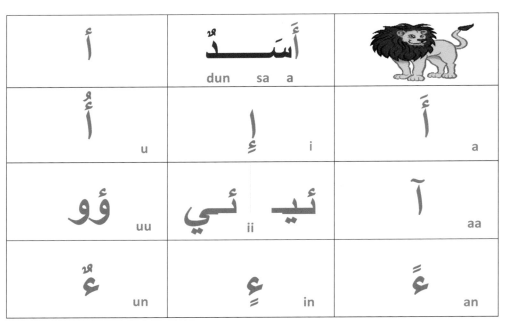

أ	أَسَـدٌ a sa dun	(صورة أسد)
أُ u	إِ i	أَ a
ؤو uu	ئـي ئـ ii	آ aa
ءٌ un	ءٍ in	ءً an

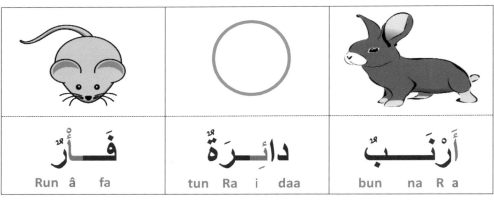

فَـأْرٌ — fa â Run

دائِـرَةٌ — daa i Ra tun

أَرْنَـبٌ — a Ra na bun

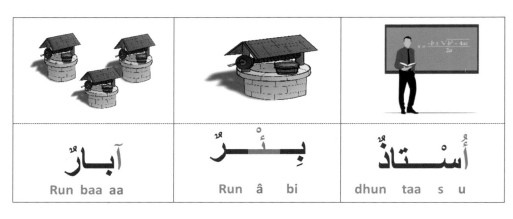

آبَارٌ — aa baa Run

بِـأْرٌ — bi â Run

أُسْـتَاذٌ — u s taa dhun

10

ب	بَقَرَةٌ tun Ra qa ba	(cow)
بُ bu	بِ bi	بَ ba
بو buu	بي ‧ بي bii	با baa
بٌ bun	بٍ bin	بًا ban

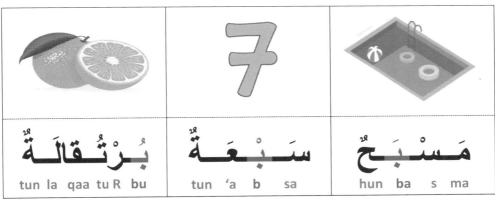

بُرْثُقَالَةٌ tun la qaa tu R bu	سَبْعَةٌ tun 'a b sa	مَسْبَحٌ hun ba s ma

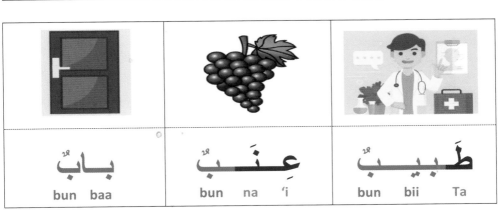

بابٌ bun baa	عِنَبٌ bun na 'i	طَبِيبٌ bun bii Ta

ت	تُفَّاحَةٌ tun ha ffaa tu	 (apple image)
تُ tu	تِ ti	تَ ta
تو tuu	تي | تِي tii	تا taa
ةٌ tun	ةٍ tin	تأً tan

توتٌ tun tuu	سَيَّارَةٌ tun Ra yyaa sa	تِبْنٌ nun b ti

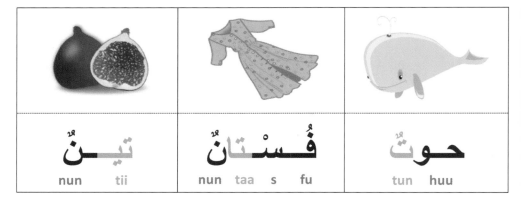

تِينٌ nun tii	فُسْتَانٌ nun taa s fu	حوتٌ tun huu

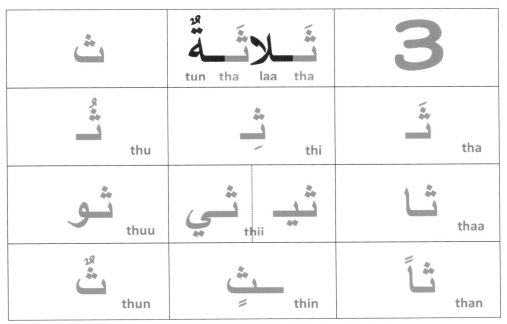

3	ثَلاثَةٌ tha laa tha tun	ثْ tha
ثُ thu	ثِ thi	ثَ tha
ثُو thuu	ثِي ثْي thii	ثا thaa
ثٌ thun	ثٍ thin	ثأ than

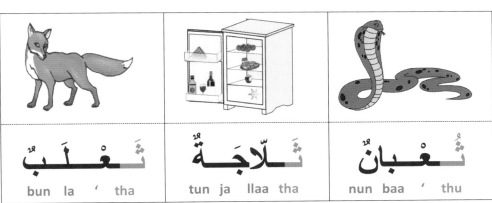

ثَعْلَبٌ tha ' la bun	ثَلاجَةٌ tha llaa ja tun	ثُعْبانٌ thu ' baa nun

ثُومٌ thuu mun	مُثَلَّثٌ mu tha lla thun	كُراثٌ ku Raa thun

جَبَلٌ ja ba lun		ج 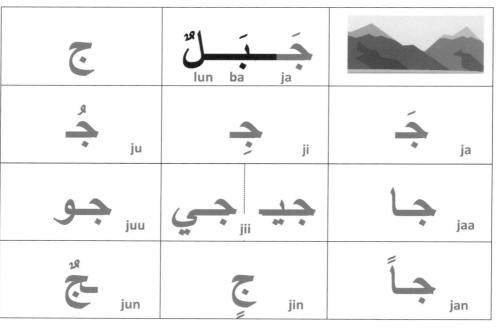
جُ ju	جِ ji	جَ ja
جو juu	جي|جي jii	جا jaa
جّ jun	جِ jin	جاً jan

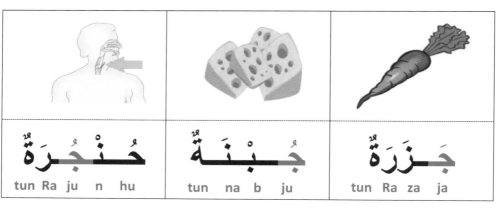

حُنْجُرَةٌ hu n ju Ra tun	جُبْنَةٌ ju b na tun	جَزَرَةٌ ja za Ra tun

نَجّارٌ na jjaa Run	إِجَّاصَةٌ i jjaa Sa tun	دَجَاجَةٌ da jaa ja tun

ح	حَمامَةٌ tun ma maa ha	
حُ hu	حِ hi	حَ ha
حو huu	حي حيـ hii	حا ha
حٌ hun	حٍ hin	حاً han

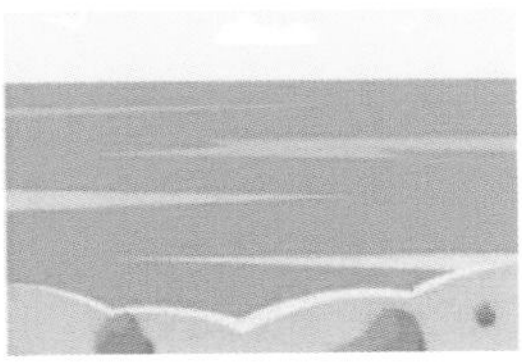		
بَحْرٌ Run h ba	حِمارٌ Run maa hi	حَلَزونٌ nun zuu la ha

	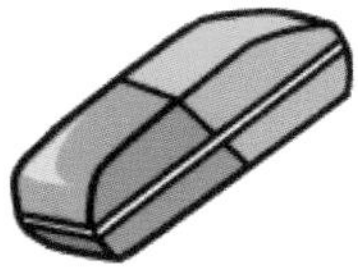	
تِمْساحٌ hun saa m ti	مِمْحاةٌ tun haa m mi	حافِلَةٌ tun la fi haa

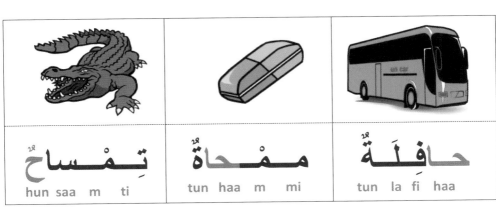

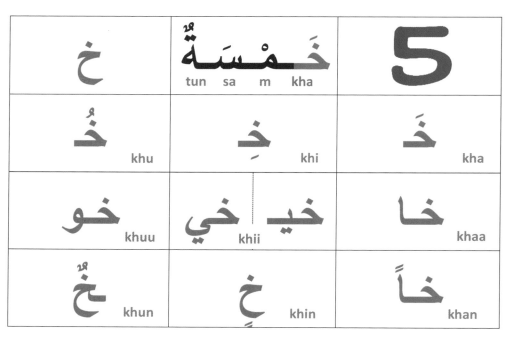

		5
خ	خَمْسَةٌ tun sa m kha	
خُ khu	خِ khi	خَ kha
خو khuu	خي خي khii	خا khaa
خّ khun	خٍ khin	خاً khan

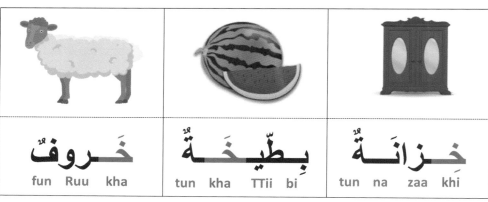

خَـرُوفٌ fun Ruu kha	بِطّيخَـةٌ tun kha TTii bi	خِـزانَـةٌ tun na zaa khi

خَـوْخٌ khun w kha	خوذَةٌ tun dha khuu	خاتَـمٌ mun ta khaa

د	دَجاجَةٌ tun ja jaa da	🐔
دُ du	دِ di	دَ da
دو duu	ديـ دي dii	دا daa
دٌّ dun	دٍ din	دَأ dan

دُبٌّ bbun du	دُخانٌ nun khaa du	دَرّاجَةٌ tun ja RRaa da

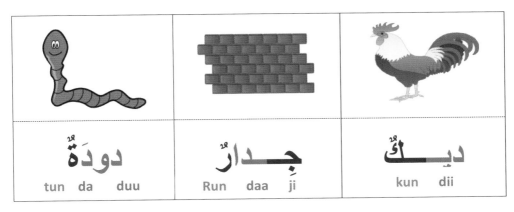

دودَةٌ tun da duu	جِدارٌ Run daa ji	ديكٌ kun dii

ذ	نُرَّةٌ tun Ra dhu	 (corn)
ذُ dhu	ذِ dhi	ذَ dha
ذو dhuu	ذي ذي dhii	ذا dhaa
ذٌّ dhun	ذٍ dhin	ذَأ dhan

ذِئْبٌ bun â dhi	ذِراعٌ 'un Raa dhi	ذُبابَةٌ tun ba baa dho

جُرَذٌ dhun Ra ju	بُذورٌ Run dhuu bu	بِذْلَةٌ tun la dh bi

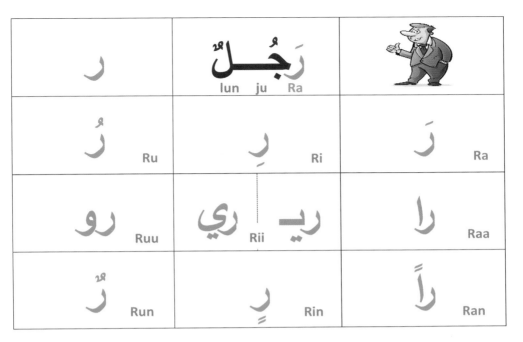

ر	رَجُلٌ lun ju Ra	
رُ Ru	رِ Ri	رَ Ra
رو Ruu	ري ـي Rii	را Raa
رٌ Run	رٍ Rin	رَا Ran

قِرْدٌ dun R qi	رُمَّانَةٌ tun na mmaa Ru	رَأْسٌ sun â Ra

سَرِيرٌ Run Rii sa	سُكَّرٌ Run kka su	فُطْرٌ Run T fu

19

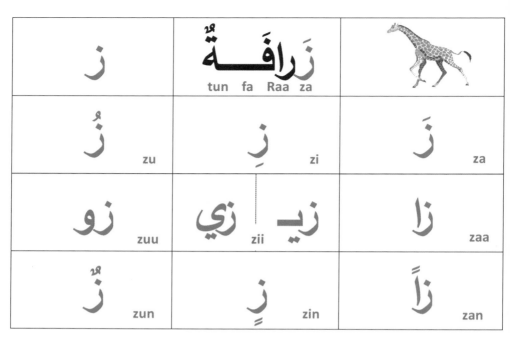

ز	زَرافَـةٌ tun fa Raa za	
زُ zu	زِ zi	زَ za
زو zuu	زيـ زي zii	زا zaa
زٌ zun	زٍ zin	زاً zan

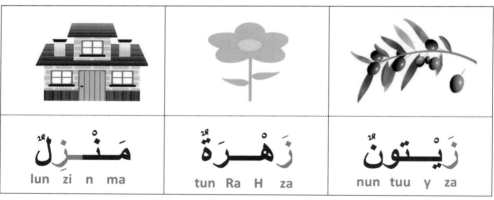

مَنْزِلٌ lun zi n ma	زَهْرَةٌ tun Ra H za	زَيْتونٌ nun tuu y za

كَرَزٌ zun Ra ka	جَزيرَةٌ tun Ra zii ja	زِرٌّ Run zi

سَمَكَةٌ tun ka ma sa	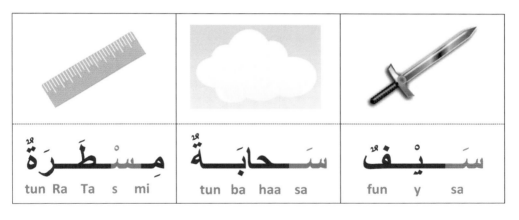	س
ـسَ sa	ـسِـ si	سُـ su
سا saa	سي سِي sii	سو suu
سأَ san	سٍ sin	سٌ sun

سَيْفٌ fun y sa	سَحابَةٌ tun ba haa sa	مِسْطَرَةٌ tun Ra Ta s mi

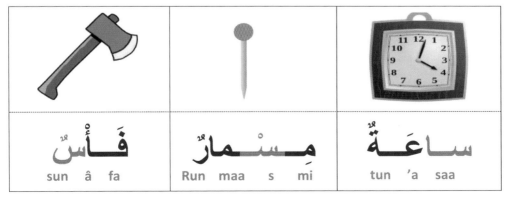

ساعَةٌ tun 'a saa	مِسْمارٌ Run maa s mi	فَأْسٌ sun â fa

21

شْ ش	شَـمْـسٌ sun m cha	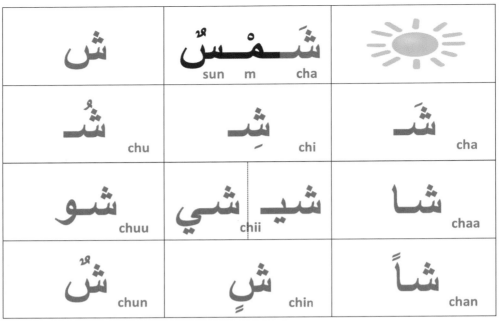
ثُـ ش chu	شِـ ش chi	شَـ ش cha
شو ش chuu	شيـ شي chii	شا ش chaa
شٌ ش chun	شٍ ش chin	شأ ش chan

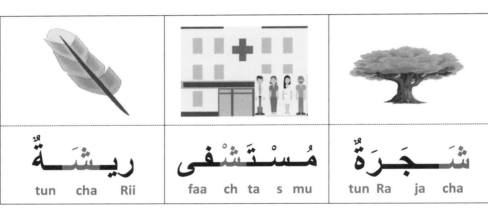

رِيـشَـةٌ tun cha Rii	مُـسْـتَـشْـفى faa ch ta s mu	شَـجَـرَةٌ tun Ra ja cha

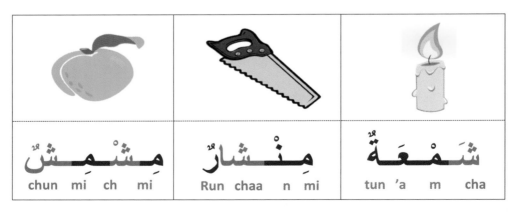

مِـشْـمِـشٌ chun mi ch mi	مِـنْـشـارٌ Run chaa n mi	شَـمْـعَـةٌ tun 'a m cha

ص	صَيّادٌ dun yyaa Sa	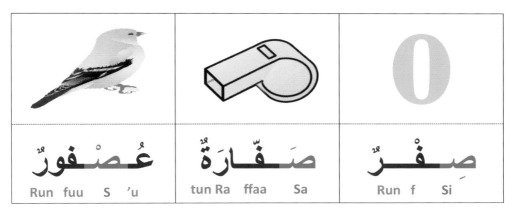
صُ Su	صِ Si	صَ Sa
صو Suu	صيد صِي Sii	صا Saa
صٌّ Sun	صٍ Sin	صأً San

عُصْفورُ Run fuu S 'u	صَفّارَةٌ tun Ra ffaa Sa	صِفْرٌ Run f Si

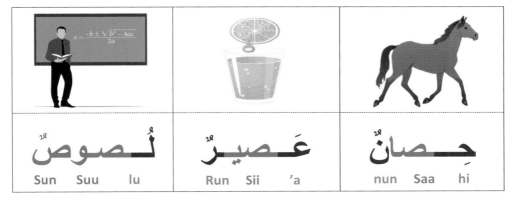

لُصوصٌ Sun Suu lu	عَصيرٌ Run Sii 'a	حِصانٌ nun Saa hi

ض	ضَفْدَعٌ ّun da f ḍi	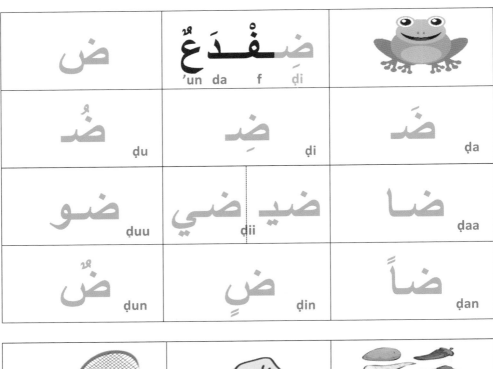
ضُ ḍu	ضِ ḍi	ضَ ḍa
ضو ḍuu	ضي ضيد ḍii	ضا ḍaa
ضٌ ḍun	ضٍ ḍin	ضاً ḍan

مِضْرَبٌ bun Ra ḍ mi	عَضَلَةٌ tun la ḍa 'a	خُضَرٌ Run ḍa khu

بَيْضٌ ḍun y ba	مُمَرِّضٌ ḍun RRi ma mu	ضِرْسٌ sun R ḍi

24

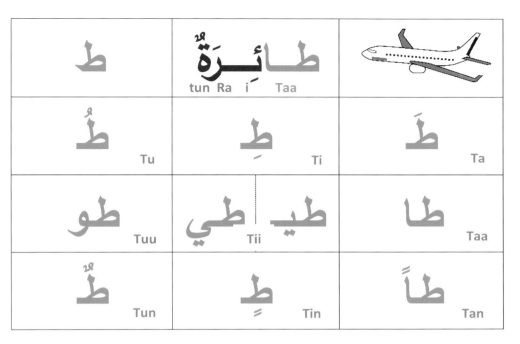

ط	طَائِرَةٌ tun Ra i Taa	
طُ Tu	طِ Ti	طَ Ta
طو Tuu	طي طي Tii	طا Taa
طٌ Tun	طٍ Tin	طاً Tan

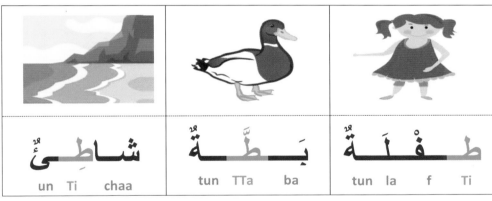

شَاطِئٌ un Ti chaa	بَطَّةٌ tun TTa ba	طِفْلَةٌ tun la f Ti

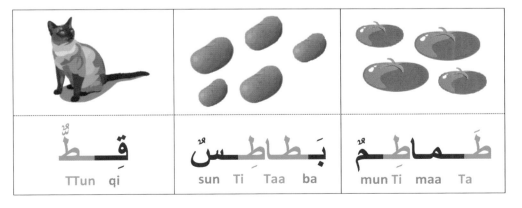

قِطٌّ TTun qi	بَطَاطِسٌ sun Ti Taa ba	طَمَاطِمٌ mun Ti maa Ta

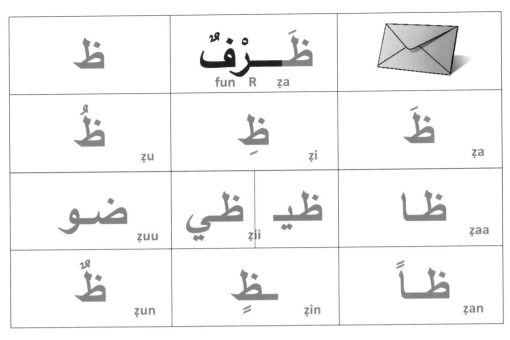

ظ	ظَـرْفٌ fun R ẓa	
ظُ ẓu	ظِ ẓi	ظَ ẓa
ضو ẓuu	ظي ظِ ẓii	ظا ẓaa
ظٌ ẓun	ظٍ ẓin	ظاً ẓan

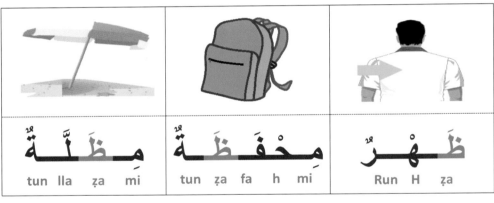

مِظَـلَّـةٌ	مِحْفَـظَـةٌ	ظَـهْرٌ
tun lla ẓa mi	tun ẓa fa h mi	Run H ẓa

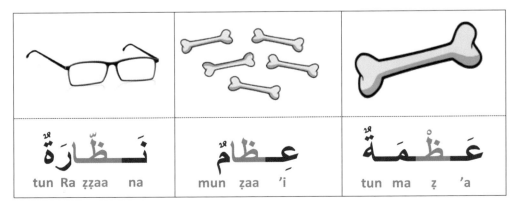

نَـظَّـارَةٌ	عِظَامٌ	عَـظْـمَـةٌ
tun Ra ẓẓaa na	mun ẓaa 'i	tun ma ẓ 'a

ع	عَيْنٌ nun y 'a	
عُ 'u	عِ 'i	عَ 'a
عو 'uu	عي عِي 'ii	عا 'aa
عٌ 'un	عٍ 'in	عاً 'an

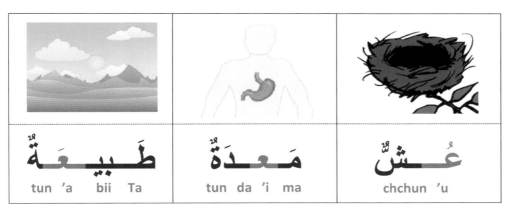

طَبِيعَةٌ tun 'a bii Ta	مَعِدَةٌ tun da 'i ma	عُشٌّ chchun 'u

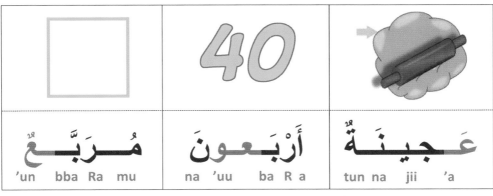

مُرَبَّعٌ 'un bba Ra mu	أَرْبَعُونَ na 'uu ba R a	عَجِينَةٌ tun na jii 'a

غ	غَابَةٌ tun ba raa_	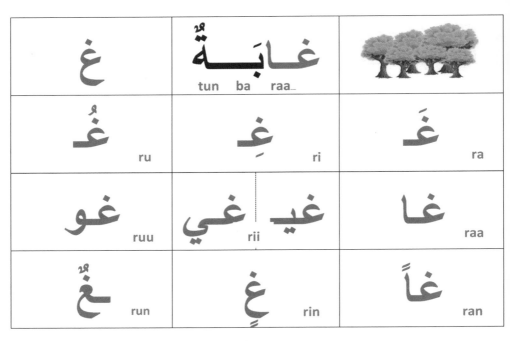
غُ ru	غِ ri	غَ ra
غو ruu	غي غي rii	غا raa
غٌ run	غٍ rin	غاً ran

غُصْنٌ nun S ru	غُرابٌ bun Raa ru	غَيْمَةٌ tun ma y ra

دِماغٌ run maa di	بَبَّغاءُ un raa bba ba	غَسَّالَةٌ tun la SSaa ra

ف	فَراشَةٌ tun cha Raa fa	(butterfly)
فُ fu	فِ fi	فَ fa
فو fuu	في فِي fii	فا faa
فٌ fun	فٍ fin	فأً fan

نافِذَةٌ tun dha fi naa	فُرْشاةٌ tun chaa R fu	فُلْفُلٌ lun fu l fu

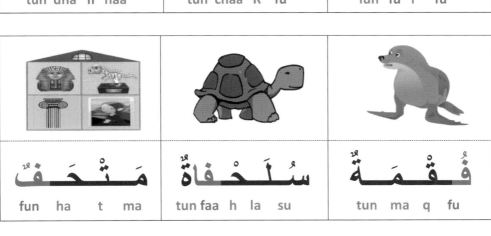

مَتْحَفٌ fun ha t ma	سُلَحْفاةٌ tun faa h la su	فُقْمَةٌ tun ma q fu

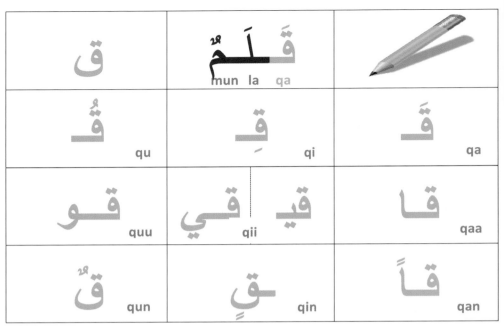

ق	قَلَمٌ mun la qa	
قُـ qu	قِـ qi	قَـ qa
ـقـو quu	قي|قي qii	قا qaa
قٌ qun	قٍـ qin	قاً qan

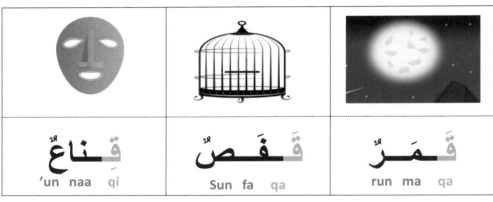

قِـنـاعٌ 'un naa qi	قَـفَـصٌ Sun fa qa	قَـمَـرٌ run ma qa

فُنْدُقٌ qun du n fu	حَقِيبَةٌ tun ba qii ha	بَرْقوقٌ qun quu R ba

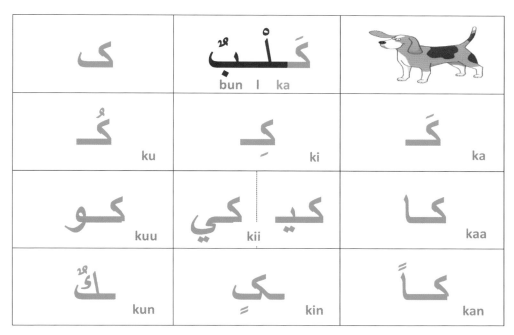

ك	كَلْبُ bun l ka	
كُ ku	كِ ki	كَ ka
كو kuu	كي كي kii	كا kaa
كُنْ kun	كِ kin	كأ kan

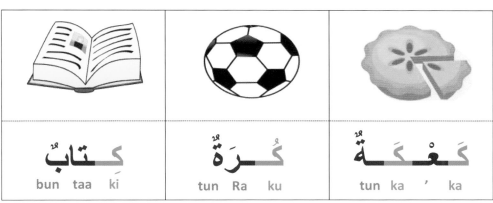

كِتابُ bun taa ki	كُرَةٌ tun Ra ku	كَعْكَةٌ tun ka ' ka

أَسْمَاكُ kun maa s a	سِكِّينْ nun kkii si	مَكْتَبُ bun ta k ma

31

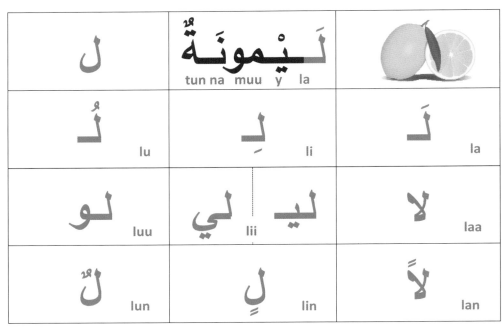

ل	لَيْمونَةٌ	 tun na muu y la

لُ lu	لِ li	لَ la
لو luu	لي | ليـ lii	لا laa
لٌ lun	لٍ lin	لاً lan

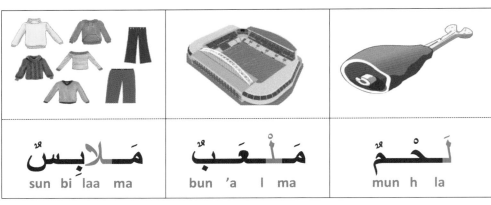

مَلابِسٌ sun bi laa ma	مَلْعَبٌ bun 'a l ma	لَحْمٌ mun h la

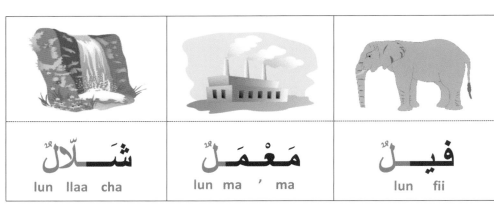

شَلّالٌ lun llaa cha	مَعْمَلٌ lun ma ' ma	فيلٌ lun fii

32

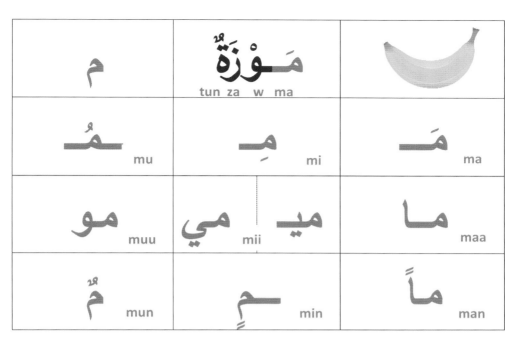

م	مَوْزَةٌ tun za w ma	(banana)
مُ mu	مِ mi	مَ ma
مو muu	مي مي mii	ما maa
مٌ mun	مٍ min	مَأ man

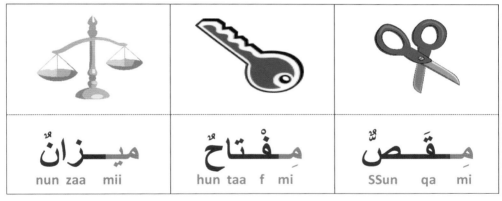

ميزانٌ nun zaa mii	مِفْتاحٌ hun taa f mi	مِقَصٌّ SSun qa mi

سُلَّمٌ mun lla su	حَمامَةٌ tun ma maa ha	ماعِزٌ zun 'i maa

ن	نَمْلَةٌ tun la m na	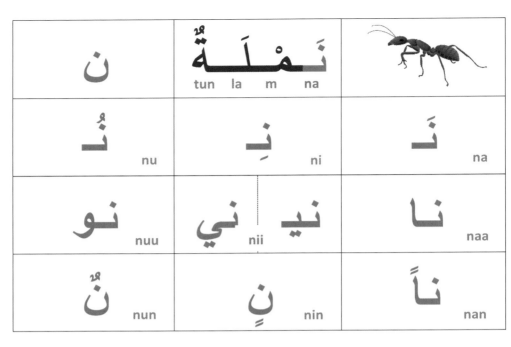
نُ nu	نِ ni	نَ na
نو nuu	ني نِي nii	نا naa
نٌ nun	نٍ nin	نأً nan

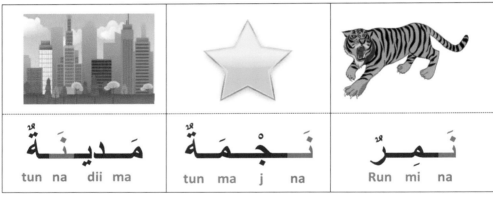

مَدِينَةٌ tun na dii ma	نَجْمَةٌ tun ma j na	نَمِرٌ Run mi na

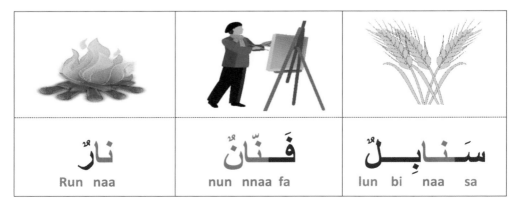

نَارٌ Run naa	فَنَّانٌ nun nnaa fa	سَنَابِلُ lun bi naa sa

هـ	دُ هُدْ dun Hu d Hu	
هُـ Hu	ـهِ Hi	ـهَ Ha
هـو Huu	هـي هـا Hii	هـا Haa
ةٌ Hun	ـهِ Hin	هـأً Han

سَـهْـمٌ mun H sa	هَـدِيَّةٌ tun yya di Ha	هَـرَمٌ mun Ra Ha

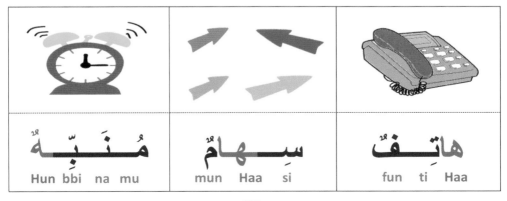

مُـنَـبِّـهٌ Hun bbi na mu	سِـهَامٌ mun Haa si	هاتِـفٌ fun ti Haa

و	وَرْدَةٌ tun da r wa	🌹
وُ wu	وِ wi	وَ wa
وو wuu	ويـ وي wii	وا waa
وٌ wun	ـوٍ win	وأً wan

خَـوْخٌ khun w kha	كَـوْكَبٌ bun ka w ka	طَاوِلَةٌ tun la wi Taa

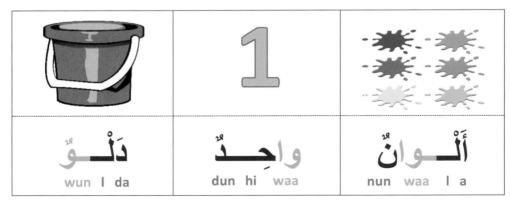

دَلْـوٌ wun l da	واحِدٌ dun hi waa	أَلْـوانٌ nun waa l a

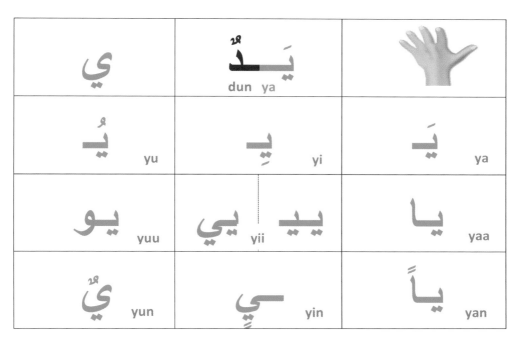

ي	يَدٌ dun ya	<img hand>
يُ yu	يِ yi	يَ ya
يو yuu	يي ييـ yii	يا yaa
يٌّ yun	ـيٍ yin	ياً yan

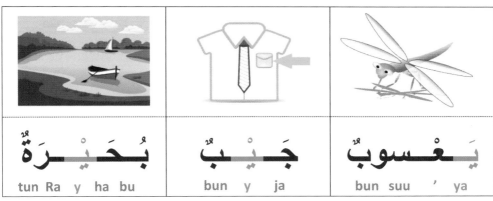

بُحَيْرَةٌ tun Ra y ha bu	جَيْبٌ bun y ja	يَعْسوبٌ bun suu ' ya

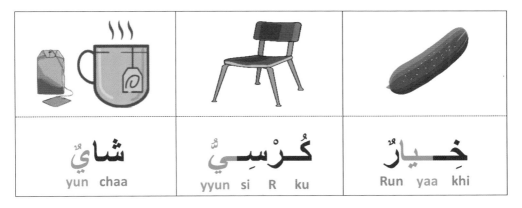

شايٌ yun chaa	كُرْسِيٌّ yyun si R ku	خِيارٌ Run yaa khi

Printed in Great Britain
by Amazon

26486505R00023